DISCOVERING DINOSAURS

by Janet Riehecky
illustrated by Helen Endres

THE CHILD'S WORLD

MANKATO, MN

Grateful appreciation is expressed to
Bret S. Beall, Research Consultant,
Field Museum of Natural History, Chicago,
Illinois, who reviewed this book to
insure its accuracy.

Library of Congress Cataloging in Publication Data

Riehecky, Janet, 1953-
    Discovering dinosaurs / by Janet Riehecky ; illustrated by Helen Endres.
        p. cm. — (Dinosaur books)
    Summary: Describes some significant dinosaur discoveries and what scientists can learn from studying dinosaur fossils.
    ISBN 0-89565-620-5 (lib. bdg.)
    1. Dinosaurs—Juvenile literature.   [1. Dinosaurs.   2. Fossils.
3. Paleontology.]   I. Endres, Helen, ill.   II. Title.   III. Series:
Riehecky, Janet, 1953-   Dinosaur books.
QE862.D5R43   1990
567.9′1—dc20   90-2507
                                                                CIP
                                                                AC

DISCOVERING DINOSAURS

Though mysteries surround the world of the dinosaurs, scientists have discovered some of what that world was like. Gentle plant eaters roamed about searching for food. Fierce meat eaters followed them, also looking for a meal.

Scientists have discovered there were many different kinds of dinosaurs. Some of them lived in herds with their own kind, working together, caring for their babies, and fighting against enemies. Others were loners.

We know many such facts about the world of the dinosaurs, but how do we know them? There were no people alive when the dinosaurs lived.

People know about dinosaurs because scientists have found fossils from them: bones, teeth, footprints, claws, and eggs which hardened into rock over millions of years. Once, people thought that the giant bones they found belonged to elephants or other known, large animals. They didn't even know that such creatures as dinosaurs ever existed. But in the 1820's, two important events occurred which led to the discovery of dinosaurs.

In 1882 a woman named Mary Ann
Mantell found some very old, very large
teeth in a pile of gravel. She showed the
teeth to her husband, Dr. Gideon Mantell,
who was interested in fossils.

Dr. Mantell had trouble telling what
creature the teeth came from. He went to
the quarry from which the gravel had

come and found more teeth and some bones. He became convinced that the teeth and bones belonged to a huge reptile, much larger than any alive at the time.

Dr. Mantell learned that the teeth his wife had found looked like those of the iguana lizard, except that they were much, much bigger. He pictured the owner of the teeth as an enormous iguana and named it Iguanodon, which means "iguana tooth."

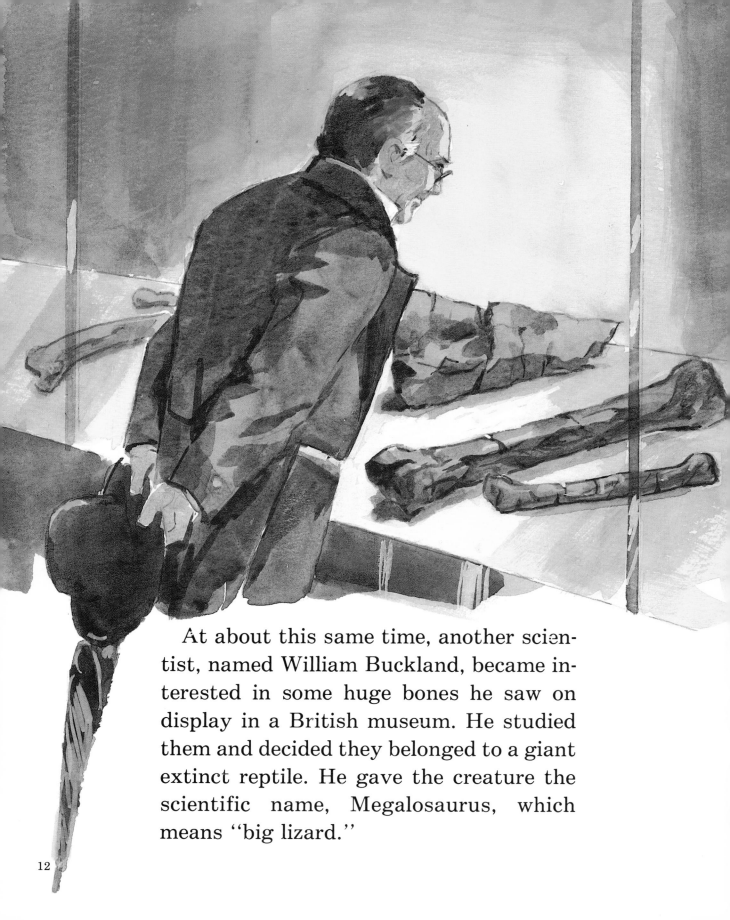

At about this same time, another scientist, named William Buckland, became interested in some huge bones he saw on display in a British museum. He studied them and decided they belonged to a giant extinct reptile. He gave the creature the scientific name, Megalosaurus, which means "big lizard."

Scientists loved the idea that huge reptiles had once lived on the earth. Eagerly they searched for more information. One scientist, Sir Richard Owen, decided these creatures needed a name. He called them dinosaurs, which means "terrible lizards."

When people heard about dinosaurs, they became just as excited as the scientists. They couldn't hear enough about them.

Scientists made life-sized models of what they thought the Iguanodon and the Megalosaurus looked like. They were put on public display in London. The scientists made many mistakes because they had only a few bones to work from. But they were so proud of their work that they had a fancy dinner party inside a half-finished model of the Iguanodon.

It took many years of study and many more discoveries before scientists found out some of the mistakes they had made. But eventually they learned that both the Iguanodon and the Megalosaurus (the first known dinosaurs) walked on two back legs, not on all fours, and that the Iguanodon had its spike on its thumb, not on its nose. They also learned that all dinosaurs held their legs straight under

them, not sprawled out to the side the way lizards do.

Through the years scientists have learned that there were many, many other types of dinosaurs. They are still discovering things about dinosaurs—and they are still correcting past mistakes. For instance, not long ago, they discovered that they had given one dinosaur two names!

17

More than a hundred years ago, scientists found bones of a giant dinosaur and named it Apatosaurus. Two years after that, they found more bones. They didn't realize those bones also belonged to an Apatosaurus, so they gave the dinosaur a new name, Brontosaurus. Because Apatosaurus was the first name given that dinosaur, that is its correct name.

Then scientists made another mistake. Both the "Brontosaurus" and the Apatosaurus were found without heads. When scientists put the bones together to make a skeleton, they used a short, thick skull that had been found miles from the other bones. It wasn't until many years later that scientists learned the Apatosaurus really had a long, slender head. It took them a hundred years to get the Apatosaurus right!

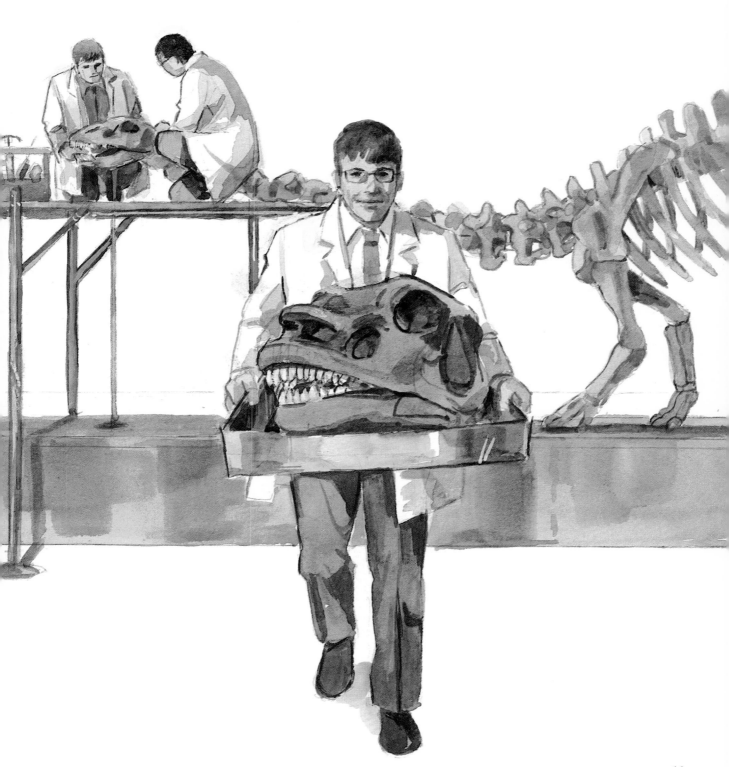

Another time they discovered that an artist had drawn a claw backward on the Hypsilophodon. This made its foot look like a bird's foot. Scientists pictured the Hypsilophodon living in trees, clinging to tree branches. When they found out the claw really faced forward, they had to move the Hypsilophodon out of the trees!

Most importantly, they have discovered that dinosaurs were not the slow, stupid, awkward animals scientists once thought they were.

Scientists know that future discoveries will probably change some of today's ideas. All the fossils they've found so far show only a small part of the world of the dinosaurs. They hope many more will be found, but most dinosaurs left no trace of themselves behind.

When a dinosaur died, other animals usually came along and ate it. If they didn't, sun, wind, and rain usually turned the dinosaur—bones and all—to dust. Wind and rain also wiped out footprints.

But, every once in a while, a dinosaur would be buried right after dying—perhaps in the mud at the bottom of a lake. As time passed, the dinosaur would be buried deeper and deeper. The soft parts of its body would still decay. But the hard parts could turn to rock if they weren't disturbed. These might lie underground for millions of years until wind and rain uncovered them, or until people dug them up.

Though this didn't happen often, it happened often enough to give scientists important information.

Scientists can put bones together and figure out where the muscles once were. This tells them what different dinosaurs looked like and how they moved.

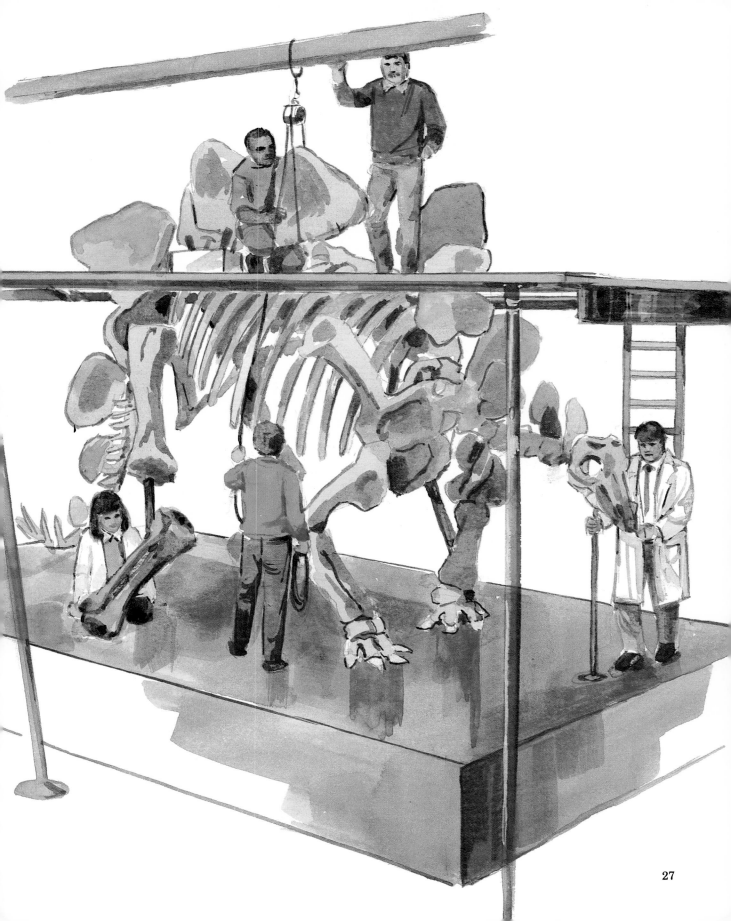

Dinosaur teeth can tell a lot too. The size and shape of the teeth tell scientists whether the dinosaur ate plants or meat or both.

Claws and horns tell how dinosaurs at-
tacked or defended themselves.

The distance between footprints tells
scientists how fast the dinosaurs could
move. And when they find footprints of
many of the same dinosaurs together,
they know that type of dinosaur traveled
in herds.

Scientists have even found fossilized
eggs and nests of dinosaurs, which have
shown us a lot about how some dinosaurs
took care of their babies.

Putting together the clues dinosaurs left behind about their world is like trying to put together a giant jigsaw puzzle with half the pieces missing. But the pieces scientists have been able to put together show us it was truly a fascinating, as well as mysterious, world.

Dinosaur Fun

Wouldn't it be exciting to go on a dinosaur dig and discover dinosaur bones? You can pretend that you are a scientist making an important discovery! You will need:

— clean chicken bones
— plaster of Paris and water (and a can to mix them in)
— a plastic or metal pan, at least 2 inches deep
— a hammer and a nail

1. Mix the plaster according to the directions on the package. Pour half of the plaster into the pan so the plaster is about ½ inch deep.
2. While the plaster is still wet, drop the chicken bones on top.
3. Pour the rest of the plaster on top of the bones to cover them.
4. When the plaster has hardened completely, turn the pan over so the plaster mold will fall out.
5. Imagine you are a scientist as you carefully chip away at the plaster with the nail and hammer to try to uncover "dinosaur" bones.

DATE DUE

0 6 III 1999			
GAYLORD			PRINTED IN U.S.A.